Bad Dog? Good Dog!

Written by
Rob Waring and **Maurice Jamall**

HEINLE
CENGAGE Learning™

Australia • Brazil • Japan • Korea • Mexico • Singapore • Spain • United Kingdom • United States

Before You Read

to hit

to take a dog for a walk

brother

dog

game

gate

meat

puppy

puppies

shopping

sister

store

street

bad

good

In the story

Yoon-Hee

Ji-Sung

Mrs. Lee

Farina

Old Woman

"Take this money, Yoon-Hee," says Mrs. Lee.
"Please go to the store with Ji-Sung."
Yoon-Hee and Ji-Sung are brother and sister.
But Ji-Sung says, "I don't want to do the shopping."
"Oh, come on, Ji-Sung," says Yoon-Hee. "Let's help Mom."

Yoon-Hee and Ji-Sung go out of the house. They walk to the store.
"I don't want to do the shopping," says Ji-Sung. "I want to play with my game."
But Yoon-Hee is not listening. She is looking at her paper.
"Eggs, meat, coffee, and milk," she says. "Come on, Ji-Sung!"

Yoon-Hee and Ji-Sung see their friend, Farina.
"Hi, Farina," says Yoon-Hee. "Do you want to come to the
store with us?"
"Sorry, no. My dog Misha has puppies now," says Farina.
"Hello, puppies," says Yoon-Hee to the dogs.
A big dog comes over to them. His name is Dingo.

"Hi, Dingo. Come here!" says Yoon-Hee.

Farina says, "Dingo wants to go for a walk. I want to take him, but . . . ,"

"Come on, Dingo," says Yoon-Hee. "Come with us."

Dingo is happy. He wants to go with Yoon-Hee and Ji-Sung.

"Thank you," says Farina. "Thank you."

Yoon-Hee, Ji-Sung, and Dingo walk to the store.
Ji-Sung is not happy. "I don't want the dog. I don't like dogs."
Yoon-Hee is angry with her brother.
"We're taking Dingo for a walk. Farina is our friend," says
Yoon-Hee.
Ji-Sung is not listening. He is playing with his game.
Yoon-Hee says, "Okay. You and Dingo wait here. I'm going into
the store."

Yoon-Hee comes back. "I have the meat," she says. "Now you go and get the milk."

Ji-Sung says, "No, you get it. I don't want to go shopping."

Yoon-Hee is angry with Ji-Sung. He is not doing the shopping. "Okay. You and Dingo wait here," she says.

Ji-Sung is playing with his game. He is not listening to Yoon-Hee.

Yoon-Hee goes into the big store.
Ji-Sung waits with Dingo. He is playing with his game.
Dingo sees the meat. He looks at Ji-Sung. Ji-Sung is not looking at Dingo.
Dingo wants the meat. He takes the meat.

Dingo runs down the street. Ji-Sung sees Dingo with the meat.

"Stop, Dingo!" says Ji-Sung.

Dingo looks at Ji-Sung, but he does not stop. Dingo runs away with the meat.

"Come here, Dingo!" says Ji-Sung. "Come here! You bad dog!"

Yoon-Hee comes out of the store. "Where's Dingo?" she asks.
"Over there," Ji-Sung says. "Sorry. He has the meat," he says.
"What? Dingo has the meat?" says Yoon-Hee. "Oh no!"
Yoon-Hee and her brother run after Dingo and the meat.

Yoon-Hee sees Dingo. "There he is," says Yoon-Hee.
"Where?" says Ji-Sung.
Yoon-Hee says, "He's there. He's at that fruit store."
Dingo is running to a woman. "Dingo, look out!" says Ji-Sung.
Dingo hits the woman.
"*Ouch*!" says the woman. She falls into the fruit.

"Dingo! Bad dog," says Yoon-Hee.

Yoon-Hee says to the woman, "I'm very sorry. Are you okay?"

Now Dingo is running into the street. He is not looking at the cars.

"Look out, Dingo!" says Ji-Sung.

"Come back!" says the man in the car. "Bad dog!" he says. "Come here!"

Dingo runs away. Yoon-Hee and Ji-Sung run after Dingo.
"Where is he now?" asks Ji-Sung.
Yoon-Hee says, "He's over there. Come on!"
Ji-Sung says, "Dingo! Come here!"
But Dingo runs and runs. Ji-Sung and Yoon-Hee run, too.

"Where's Dingo going?" asks Ji-Sung.
"He's going back to Farina's house," says Yoon-Hee. "He's at the gate."
Dingo jumps over the gate.
Yoon-Hee says, "Look. There's Farina."

Farina sees Yoon-Hee and Ji-Sung.

Dingo gives the meat to the puppies. They eat the meat.

Dingo is happy now.

"You are a very bad dog, Dingo," says Ji-Sung.

Yoon-Hee smiles. She says, "Yes, but you are a very good father!"